THE SPIRITUAL TASKS OF THE HOMEMAKER

THE SPIRITUAL TASKS OF THE HOMEMAKER

Manfred Schmidt-Brabant

TEMPLE LODGE

Translated by Carol Brousseau

The first three chapters of this book are transcripts from lectures held 16–17 May 1992 during the conference for homemakers at the Goetheanum, edited by the *Verlag am Goetheanum*. Chapter 4 is a condensation of lectures held at the village community Lautenbach in 1986, edited by the *Verlag am Goetheanum*.

Temple Lodge Publishing
Hillside House, The Square
Forest Row, RH18 5ES

Published by Temple Lodge 1996
Reprinted 1998, 2001, 2004

Originally published in German under the title *Spirituelle Grundlagen einer menschengemässen Hausmütterarbeit* by Verlag am Goetheanum, Dornach, Switzerland, 1993

A catalogue record for this book is available from the British Library

ISBN 0 904693 84 8

Cover: art by Christiana Bryan; layout by S. Gulbekian
Typeset by DP Photosetting, Aylesbury, Bucks.
Printed and bound by Cromwell Press Limited, Trowbridge, Wilts.

Contents

1
A New Vocation: Homemaker

What is to become of the family? What is to become of the home, which has been the foundation of society for centuries? Will it disintegrate? Or can it be taken hold of in a new way?

The gathering at which these questions were raised was a pilot conference; it was an attempt to discover what might be involved in grappling with the question of homemaking. We took the workplace itself as our starting-point.

In the decades since anthroposophy began, some well-founded respected career portraits have been worked out. Often these had first been inspired by Rudolf Steiner; he held whole lecture cycles about them. Have there been studies of the inner conditions of working in the home? What processes are essential, what are the secrets of this special task found all over the world? What is its significance today? What influence does it have on society? And what are the conditions involved?

Individuality and Role Expectations

The human being is not a unity. He is divided into body, soul and spirit. His spirit (his ego, his individuality) only gradually came to development in the course of human history. Only gradually did he become independent and individual.

In ancient times individuality played a minor role or no role at all. Instead there were norms. These arose because human beings were bound up with large generic groups by way of their body and soul (insofar as the soul was connected with the body). The human being was a group being, a 'group-soul being'. As a man or a woman he or she belonged to a certain sex. As a Bayer, Thüringer or Sachsener he belonged to a certain tribe or family. As a German, Italian or Dutch person he was of a particular nation. Finally, he was also part of a religious group.

His body brought him into connection with certain groups. These groups determined the norms by which he lived. In the case of the sexes this was very pronounced. What a man or a woman did was determined by their sex. The role expectations that still persist today arose under such conditions.

Gradually, during the course of history, the spiritual aspect of the human being developed. The individual, the ego, became more and more autonomous; it began to emancipate itself. In the twentieth century finally, great conflicts arose between the individual and the old role expectations. The individual felt that his life should not be determined by the role expectations of society, but by himself alone.

Humanity is still in the midst of this conflict. The battle is not yet decided, for the relevant principles remain unclear. Perhaps this is one of the reasons why the question of the homemaker has not been taken up in all the many years of anthroposophical work. Perhaps the role expectations within anthroposophical circles are still so great that until now no one has dared to take it up.

But it is overdue. We have only to glance at society to see this. Will the individual with her right to self-determination, her right to form her own life, be able to assert herself, or will the old role expectations remain and overwhelm her?

The following must be taken into account here: the fact that the human being goes through repeated earth lives and in doing so experiences different situations and genders. The eternal individuality, which gradually wrested itself from its bodily nature, is neither male nor female, neither French nor Italian, belongs to no particular religious community; this eternal individuality rises again and again out of the depths of its own becoming, to experience new and different situations.

If a person takes such a view seriously, then he accepts himself in his current life and situation. For in the next life he will live within other circumstances. This acceptance, however, is practically indispensable if a person wishes to gain a firm point of view regarding the conflict between role expectations and the assertion of the individual. For if he sees his ego, his individuality, as being only temporarily within a certain situation, then he is not tied up with it existentially. It is merely his current garment, his current body, his current task. This view enables him to meet expectations and make choices from out of his individuality.

It has rightly often been said that the independence of an individual is only as strong as his ability to at least feel that he is not identical with his body—and thus not with his gender, sex, race, nor folk either.

This is also the starting-point for all homemaker issues, and it will become ever more urgent: a homemaker is an individual who enters such work for particular reasons.

Usually the homemaker will start out with naive ideals, ones that she has built up herself or which approach her as role expectations from outside—described by the words a 'good mother', a 'good homemaker'. Where does this ideal come from? In Middle Europe we connect certain concepts with the word 'good'. However, since we live in a pluralist world society, the Middle European ideal is not the only one. Other cultures have other role expectations and also other ideals.

Even within European society there are differences. What was the ideal for an aristocratic woman in the previous century? She was supposed to be a lady of society, to be able to ride, to be accomplished in the arts. Servants were responsible for the household and children. This was thus an ideal which does not correspond to our current one.

Country women had other ideals. Their role expectations came from the village community.

The ideal of a 'good wife and mother' comes from middle-class society of the previous century in Middle Europe. It stems from a time in which the housewife did not have to care for the household by herself. Cooks took care of the meals, nursemaids looked after the children.

Such conditions continued until about the beginning of this century. However, today's role expectations are still based on those past social conditions even though they have since changed. Today the household rests with the homemaker alone.

Let us take our starting-point from today's totally overtaxed homemaker. She neither lives up to her ideals nor does she fulfill the expectations of her family. This is at the root of her great frustration, and it is tearing the family apart and destroying it.

Overstrain is always at the bottom of things. The homemaker has a significant amount of work to do which she can hardly manage physically. A deep hopelessness arises, leading to loneliness. Children, kitchen and expectations; she feels isolated with these tasks. In addition there is the lack of inner stimulation; while she is doing (apparently) boring things, the rest of the world remains closed to her. Furthermore her bad conscience plagues her, for her ideal is unachievable. A feeling of meaninglessness takes hold. This is paired with the longing deep in her soul for meaning in her everyday work, for freedom—also a longing for love, which raises life onto a higher plane.

Millions of women and homemakers know these frustrations. They live with them—or they don't. For this is where they begin to look for a way out. As a rule young women learn an occupation which they then give up because of marriage and children. Their first occupation is replaced by the second, homemaking, leading to the frustration described. Often women break out of the family as soon as the children are big and return to their first occupation, fleeing their isolation. Another method is divorce. If a divorce happens by the choice of the wife, there is often such an escape at the root of it. A third possibility is an inner emigration into illness, depression or alcohol.

But there are also other ways of overcoming frustrations: reform. The attempt to do this is as old as our century; reforms began already in the first decade of the twentieth century. Health food and alternative clothing appeared, a different way of raising children was tried (today we would speak of anti-authoritarian methods). The emancipation of women began: women became politically active, broke out of their families (without deserting them however) and became engaged in major world concerns.

It is evident from the whole wealth of these events that women tried to overcome the frustration caused by role expectations—by protesting about it individually. They also sought to build a sense of community in their homes using new forms such as the extended family and the kibbutz, which continue today.

The extended family would rent an apartment or house together, thereby overcoming the isolation, easing some of the workload and avoiding loneliness. The negative experiences of the homemaker were dispersed. The extended family and kibbutz are attempts to overcome out-of-date and impossible role expectations in respect of the single family, and to prevent the catastrophic results in the soul of the homemaker.

Strength and Insight

Similar problems confronted also those homemakers who came across anthroposophy at the beginning of the century.

If we think of Rudolf Steiner's Mystery Dramas we get a peculiar picture: he introduced them with a prologue in which two women speak about their lives. One is an anthroposophist, the other is critical of spiritual science. During the conversation the anthroposophical mother, Sophia, tries to explain what ideas she unites with her life as a mother: 'Just as little as seed forces *teach* the plant how to grow, but rather appear as living beings within it, so our ideas don't *teach*: they pour themselves, igniting life—giving life—into our being.' Now comes the crucial sentence: 'Everything that makes life seem meaningful to me I owe to the thoughts that have become available to me. I owe to them not only the courage but also the *insight* and the *strength* that let me hope to make my children into people who are not only industrious and fit for outward life in the usual sense but who will carry inner peace and satisfaction in their souls.' In the manuscript the two words 'insight' and 'strength' are underlined. (See Rudolf Steiner, *The Portal of Initiation*.)

How does one find the strength to manage, how does one find the insight?

This motif was important to Steiner. In an earlier draft of this scene the conversation takes place between a married couple. In this case the skeptic is the husband, and during their discussion his wife says:

In everything your education offered women,
I used to lack the courage to raise the children.
You yourself have long since realized
that it is only thanks to this spiritual view
that I have not only the courage,
but more—the insight and strength.

Thus we find 'strength' and 'insight' already in the earlier draft. And these are what matter, if the household is to be handled from out of the individuality and not according to old role expectations.

Belonging to the question of how to develop strength and insight is the question of reincarnation.

Remember: the human being is an individuality. He is neither man nor woman; he is *in* either a male or female body at present. This gives him certain tasks to fulfil which come to him from destiny. In befriending anthroposophical thinking it is assumed that one's destiny was not only chosen, but in a certain sense also prepared. One chooses this life for oneself. An individuality that incorporates herself as a homemaker could also have become a man. But she became a woman. She formed her destiny so that she became a wife and mother. What did she want to achieve by it?

This is an abstract question at first. But it is one of the most central questions of humanity today. With many other occupations, it is easy to understand the karma involved. It is easy for a pediatrician to say that she became a doctor because she wanted to heal the sick. But what does a mother with children want? What effect does the homemaker have on the course of history?

The New Mysteries

Let us look back to the time of the ancient Mysteries, to the time that had its last echoes in ancient Greece, and its culmination in ancient Egypt, Babylon, Persia and India. In those days, everything was determined by the Mystery temples and Mystery places. A pluralist, liberal life was still unknown; things were extremely strict and rigorous.

Our freedom, which we take for granted today, did not exist then. Harvest time and sowing time were controlled, as were what we today call the sphere of religion and learning: rites, customs and education.

The Mystery centres influenced household life right down to details. From these holy places all of the affairs of humanity—which had not yet come of age—were guided. Matters of science and religion were taught, and guidance was given for the arts and occupations.

For the people of that time the supersensible world was still open. They lived with powerful, dreamy, imaginative pictures and were thus able to experience that each of the Mystery centres was inspired by a certain planet. In each of the Mysteries different priorities were developed. All of these elements were held together by the sun. From Venus came everything connected with play and enjoyment. Mars inspired everything connected with war. Mercury gave impulses for communication. Saturn determined the inner space, the living space of the human being. Jupiter was there when roles and tasks were distributed. The moon, finally, determined everything connected with physical enjoyment—from nourishment to sexuality.

Originally, these Mysteries gave the inspiration for everything. Everything connected with the household was influenced by spiritual concerns. All aspects of it were originally gifts of the gods. For the sake of the freedom of mankind, the Mysteries had to come to an end. This began in Greece; instead of Delphi, Ephesus and Samothrace—the last great Mysteries—came Plato and Aristotle. They represent independently thinking human beings. The emancipation of the individual began with the logic of Aristotle. Today the individual is free—can be free—if he wants to be.

When he was no longer determined by the gods, the human being began to establish himself as an earth being. The gods still worked within the religious element, but directions as to how the earth was to be formed in a human way were no longer given. That had been the content of the Mysteries. The Mysteries had led human beings to become ever more human and differentiated—to develop the arts, the sciences, social life and forms of civilization.

As independence developed, the demise of old civilizations and cultural forms began—especially during the last centuries. Today nothing can be managed with the old forces. The old ideals and role expectations are used up, no longer carry—neither for men nor women. New Mysteries need to arise in society.

The old Mysteries went under; they existed only so long as the human being was 'under age'. The new Mysteries have to reckon with an individual ego that has become independent.

In the Egyptian epoch everything was still connected. The entire culture was an organic whole: a Mystery culture. The new Mysteries should become a Mystery culture also. All aspects of civilization and culture should become an organic whole.

Since the human being is now emancipated, he can no longer expect directions from above. There are no temples any more that give such directions. Neither can the Goetheanum be expected to give directions. Only the individual is left. And the place to start is in the household. The new Mystery society will start with the household—or not at all. For where homemakers are working out of spiritual understanding that is where the new society will arise.

Governments, the Vatican, also the Goetheanum, can relay insights. But the new Mysteries arise individually at various places; they arise when households that are spiritualizing themselves join together and then work further into education, health, etc.

If the homemaker asks after the purpose of her work, the answer is: she stands within the situations from out of which a new society will develop. Therefore 'homemaker' in the future will receive a totally new meaning, particularly with regard to the role of the woman. For the homemaker's whole existence stands at the centre of one of the greatest changes ever to take place in human history.

Extremely dark conditions were prophesied by Rudolf

Steiner for our current civilization. He said openly that by the end of the century Europe would stand before an abyss, if our way of living did not change. But he said also that if enough individuals wanted it, a renewal of civilization would be possible. That is why he said again and again that humanity must learn to include the spiritual element, the principle of initiation, among the principles of civilization. To express it differently: just as in the ancient Mysteries, humanity must learn—but now independently—to place in its centre a principle of order that connects everything. This alone can be the guiding principle for the modern home-maker.

This principle of initiation or individualization means to make things more human; the human being is neither a bodily being nor a species being but a spiritual being. Why does the human being assert his individuality now? The answer lies in the words 'love' and 'freedom'. The interaction of freedom and love is what makes up an individuality. If the human being were only free, everything would end in chaos; if he had only love, everything would become force. Freedom and love, mutually fructifying each other, are ordering principles that civilization needs once again.

The household is the starting-point. The family life of father, mother and child is the smallest and most basic part of our social life. That is where the renewal must make a small beginning.

Europe as a continent of freedom, as a continent of love, will not arise in Brussels and not in Berlin; such a Europe will come from the individually formed primal element of society: the home, the family, the homemaker. How can the homemaker find the strength for this task? Is there a path of development for homemakers? Are there exercises that help one to organize, relieve time pressure and plan well? And how does the homemaker find new insight?

2
The Life-organism of the Household

The whole problem of the smallest element of society, the family and household, can only be solved from a particular point of view: the idea of the closed organism. Here is an example from life. How difficult it is for a small child to learn to walk. How strenuous it is to carry out different movements simultaneously! But once the child has learned it, once it can co-ordinate those different movements, then it no longer thinks of its earlier difficulties. A more technical example is driving. How chaotic the first driving lessons were. But once one has mastered it, one no longer thinks of the separate activities; the whole series of movements, from watching the traffic to the simultaneous use of brake and gear shift, has become an organic whole (as far as this can be said for a technical area).

The same organic unity used to exist centuries ago in households. The entire household used to be managed painlessly from out of the old forces. This was determined not by consciousness but by instinct. Much was passed on instinctively from mother to daughter, from grandmother to granddaughter. Women did not work out of their individualities. What they did was carried by forces of the past, by instincts and traditions, which gave the separate elements their proper relationship. In everyday life everything had its place—eating, cleaning and order, play, social contacts, business contacts, inner quiet, were all formed by these instincts for living. The family was still a totally human organism.

Since the beginning of the century—and especially after 1945—the instinctive handling of household life diminished; it was lost by young homemakers, and many were helpless. Instead of hereditary impulses and the workings of the group soul, now emancipation and individuality determined their lives.

Humanity still stands within this situation today. In particular European humanity must stop and think about the manifold related functions of the household. But this is only possible by looking at it in a new way. Today the human being can only achieve such a new point of view by means of knowledge and consciousness—what for the ancients came unconsciously.

Aspects of the Household

Adults understand the child according to the many levels of its being. Besides the physical body it forms a life body, an etheric body; with puberty the astral element, the astral body, becomes free; at the end of the third cycle of seven years its individuality is apparent—the human being has come of age.

This way of looking at the human being is a basic concept of anthroposophical knowledge. The world around the human being is to be understood on different levels as well: a physical, an etheric, an astral, and finally a spiritual level. These levels are found in the human being and nature, in the social life and in the smallest building stone of society— the family, the home.

Thus the household includes these different aspects:

1. The physical body; the physical aspects of the living space, the surroundings, etc.
2. The etheric being, revealed in the various activities and in the forming of the living community. An example of these etheric forces might be that a more phlegmatic or choleric temperament tends to predominate, irrespective of the temperaments of the individual people.

3. The astral element; the astral body, in which all the feeling, willing and thinking live. These qualities are carried by the community's individuals.
4. The spirit-self; the spiritualized astral body. This spiritual being belongs to the region of the angels; one could call it the actual spiritual element of a household.

The household with its individuals is thus an organism having higher members. It can only be mastered by way of consciously living with these members. The homemaker has to know which elements in her household need to be brought together and how, in order for an atmosphere to arise in which the family members—according to their individual natures—can be human. In this there is no right or wrong. This is part of the transition to individuality; the homemaker has to find what suits *her* family.

One thing, however, is a fact: consciousness. Consciousness must be developed. If the homemaker thinks about her household, if she asks herself questions about it, then she begins to sharpen her consciousness for these matters. She begins to take hold of a further bit of her sphere of work.

Etheric Body

Belonging to the aspect of the etheric processes are etheric beings, or, as they used to be called, elemental beings. In the previous century it was usual in the evenings to put out a bowl of milk for the house spirit—an expression of the homemaker's belief in invisible helpers. One should not have an all too anthropomorphic picture of these beings, however—but one should not completely ignore them either. For the elemental world is everywhere where there are processes going on within matter.

Today it is difficult to approach this fact. With our thinking which has become abstract it is hardly possible to understand what in those days used to be more of an expression of the feelings. And yet nothing is truer than the tale of the Brownie of Cologne (a story by August Kopisch). For a deep folk wisdom was expressed there: that elemental beings used to help in the household.

Of course we shouldn't imagine this all too materialistically. A sewing job was not found finished the next morning. But invisible forces—elemental helping forces—made the housework easier. Why do they not help us today? One homemaker was too curious, as the saying goes. She wanted to see her helpers, so she scattered peas. When the elemental beings came, they slipped on the peas, and tumbled all over each other. Angry, they went away and never came back!

This legend points to something important: it is not curiosity that is to be revived, but our relationship to the world of elemental beings. This is not easy because factual functional thinking—acquired in the last centuries by means of the sciences—cannot be applied directly to the higher worlds.

The etheric world does not consist of solid, measurable, graspable aspects, but rather of processes, movement and interpenetration. It is thus not a world of things but of living beings. If one enters it one becomes aware that it is only in the physical world that things appear lifeless. For wherever material is handled, there are processes. Rudolf Steiner gave an often cited example: to the homemaker who complained to him that her household responsibilities gave her no time to read his lecture cycles he answered gravely, 'When you clean your living room, you release elemental beings. When you read a lecture cycle, you release no elemental beings.' This means that cleaning has an influence. Everywhere where dirt gathers elemental beings are held fast. For them the moist cloth means release.

This is practical occultism. Without it the homemaker will not be able to cope with her household. If she can connect herself to the elemental world, she will find a new approach to her work.

Astral Body

In addition to the etheric body the household has an astral body. This is a very different world. It is the realm of soul; it is palpable in the climate, in the aura of a household.

The astral body can be designated as the third member of a household; it arises through the activity of the people there. Artistic activities are an example of what influences the climate. Humour also affects it—to which Rudolf Steiner attached much importance. Humour has unlimited importance. In the second half of Earth evolution it will take the place that was held by piety until now. Piety and humour allow the human being to raise himself above himself. Only someone who can laugh about himself has humour. Laughing at others only is not true humour, but to have humour means to lift oneself above the dichotomies of the world. Of course this can still happen through piety today, if one acknowledges one's imperfections.

It is said of the adversary powers that they cannot laugh. Lucifer cannot laugh and Ahriman can only be ironic and sarcastic. True humour is Christian. This is an area already bordering on the spirit: if humour is truly present, then a certain cheerfulness lives in the household. And here too one comes into a world of beings. These are even more important than the elemental beings, for they live on a higher level.

Elemental beings, the helping spirits, make the work easier. The soul-beings or penates are the guarding spirits of houses, known already in ancient Rome. They relate to the house and to the community in it as the guardian angel does to the human being. The penates stand among the angels, but there are more of them.

Spirituality

The fourth, most important level is the spiritual one. A certain spirituality lives in every house, determined for example by the religious life. A certain tone is established through one's religion and philosophy of life. Important here is the question of 'how'. How does a family live with the elements of culture? How are questions of knowledge, art, the religious life and human relationships handled? Only with the spirituality in a household is the organism complete.

Beyond that the homemaker is aware of the angels: her own angel, the angel of her husband, those of her children. For each person has an angel. Everyone has a guardian angel who guides him through life and brings about his karma.

These angels—spiritual beings—enter into the life of a household. This is true also of deceased members of the family. The spirit of a house is just as open for the spiritual world as the etheric is open for the elemental world. The homemakers of old had an instinctive knowledge of the helping elemental beings, of the protecting penates and the spirituality of a household, which the human being today has lost.

But since the household organism is a real world, the human being can and must acquire this knowledge again. For these beings live in processes, live in events. And the homemaker stands in the midst of such events. For housework consists of processes of different kinds, and in these jobs the homemaker continually influences the life-spheres of elemental beings. If she experiences the household as an organism, then she has an initial basis for a path of knowledge. She revitalizes her work through thinking about it each day. Processes, which had been unconscious before, now become visible—she begins to wake up.

In anthroposophy we speak of two great spiritual powers

that try to disturb our balance: Lucifer and Ahriman. The luciferic forces lead the human being away from earthly life, detach him from obligations. The ahrimanic powers force the human being into a form, bind him fast. Ahriman is the solidifying, Lucifer the dissolving element.

These two powers are everywhere where human qualities are, thus also in the household. Lucifer and Ahriman are continually pulling to the one side or the other. But the human being or the representative of mankind develops his ego, his individuality, by keeping these forces in balance. This is the primal motif of human existence. A homemaker who wants to be a 'good mother', a 'good wife', essentially wants to create a *human* household. To run a household in a human way means to see through Lucifer and Ahriman. Luciferic and ahrimanic distortions within the household begin with simple structural problems: everything can disintegrate into chaos—or end up in sterile order.

But balance has to be maintained, a middle ground found. Here the question begins to arise in us—and anthroposophical insight is necessary for it—how does 'absolute' order affect the soul, how chaos? While poverty of the soul comes from the first, an overtaxing of the etheric body is caused by the second.

A different example: emptiness and abundance. There are people who crowd their homes with objects; others prefer an extremely simple decor. In an empty room, memories of past incarnations can rise up, for everywhere where there is a lack of objects the imagination blooms inwardly. Abundance on the other hand can have an inspiring effect.

Here, too, it is a matter of two form principles which have to be brought into balance.

Matter

Let us go from Lucifer and Ahriman, from order and chaos, from elemental beings and angels, back to the physical body—to matter. The world of matter has a strong relationship to the will-nature of the human being. Matter is divided by way of its relationship to the will. Three kinds of matter dominate in the household: food, textiles, and the solid materials such as wood, glass and stone. These materials have a particular relationship to people. Solid material has a relationship to knowledge, while textiles are related to the rhythmic element and the feelings.

First of all the textiles: we differentiate between plant material (cotton, linen) and animal material (wool, silk). These four kinds of material are related to four areas: cotton has a relationship to the physical, linen to the etheric, wool to the soul, and silk to the ego.

The handling of textiles can vary widely. One person prefers glass and chrome, another wood and cloth. Here, too, there is no right or wrong—only what is right for the individual.

Foodstuffs have an inner order of their own as well. In anthroposophical nutrition it is not only the healthiness of food that plays a role. Important also is the process surrounding the product—the growth process, the participation of human and elemental beings. Until now our attention has been given too much to matter as such. One of the great cultural achievements of mankind has been overlooked: the art of cooking. This art was developed in the monasteries of the Middle Ages. The art of cooking is the humanization of products; preparing the food is an etheric process. The art of cooking has been neglected. The many anthroposophical cookbooks do not change this fact. For there is hardly a cookbook that mentions this etheric process. In the art of cooking many secrets occur; it is a mysterious etheric-alchemistic process. This artistic feeling in dealing with food lies within the potential of every homemaker.

Living in the Home

Belonging to life in the home are three elements: light, warmth and power. It used to be that particular soul qualities arose in connection with them.

Now the situation has changed completely. A wealth of initiative and will-expression has been taken away from the human being by electricity. Not for nothing did Rudolf Steiner remind the members in his last words of the dangers connected with electricity (see Rudolf Steiner, *Leading Thoughts*, March 1925).* For electricity creates a relationship to subnature; it can only be balanced out by means of the supersensible.

This does not mean that we should flee the gains of technical science. Rather, it is important to find out how things work, in order to create a balance.

Light: It used to be that inner and outer light were one. When it became dark, a candle was lit. People sat around the light; it was a precious thing. And something enlightening always radiated from it. Today light can be had without effort by pressing a button. We can take light for granted; an unconscious and loveless relationship arises.

Warmth: It used to be that warmth only entered the home if something was burned. Usually a home had only one fireplace. People gathered around the fire—a place of warmth, a place, too, which spoke to their feelings. Today we can handle warmth just as carelessly as light. As a result, the ability to develop differentiated experiences is reduced here too.

---

* *Anthroposophical Leading Thoughts* (London: Rudolf Steiner Press 1973).

Power: For a long time power was available only in the form of manual work. Windmills and waterwheels did produce energy, but in the household people had to rely on their own strength. When electricity became available the situation changed; countless machines make the work easier.

We cannot do without electricity any more. But we must create a way of compensating inwardly for what has been lost through external aids.

The household is actually an alchemistic laboratory. What did the ancients actually mean by this concept? *Labora* means 'work'. The household therefore was a work place where material was given a human cast in manifold ways. This was the great ideal of the Rosicrucians, the great Rosicrucian impulse of the Middle Ages: to take hold of the material world in order to make it more human, more spiritual.

This cultural impulse, founded in the Middle Ages by Christian Rosenkreutz himself, is the basis today for the new Mysteries in the new, spiritually oriented households. Households that become conscious of this process stand right in the middle of the Rosicrucian stream.

Thus the path of development of the homemaker is a Rosicrucian path. Today a path of knowledge has to be one that can be carried out within every kind of career. The Rosicrucian path does not require withdrawal from life. In fact it can only blossom fully if the human being stands in the midst of life, in the midst of the transformation and recasting of life. And nowhere is this more many-sided and universal than in the household. This is why the household is the point of departure for the new Mysteries.

3
Seed of the New Mystery Society

All human activity takes place within a certain tension. This arises between the ideal—a career ideal, a life ideal, or a religious ideal—and the impossibility of living up to it. Only the human being lives within such a tension. Animals of course do not; searching for food, play and reproduction constitute a closed organism for the animal which is all it needs. But the human being creates pictures—ideals. He tries to follow them as he grapples with himself and the world. All working people have their ideals. Also the homemaker has ideals, which she wants to meet according to her individual abilities.

Many problems of the homemaker arise from the initial inability to live up to such ideals. But much needs to be altered regarding the homemaker ideal, as we have already seen. A contemporary homemaker can no longer fulfil the role expectations of the old days. New ideals are necessary, they should be individual and obvious. If a homemaker wants to achieve an ideal, then she must see the validity in it and be able to accept it. Only then will she want to make the free decision to strive for it.

More important than the question of the ideal is the question of strength. How does a person actually learn the homemaker career? One doesn't become a mother through taking a training. Of course there are home economic schools, where young ladies learn to cook and iron. But the inner task of the homemaker has to be acquired independently. The training in homemaking is individual; it comes about during the course of the individual homemaker's life.

At the time of the Mysteries, the spirit element was *brought* to humanity. People were trained by teachers.

Universities are a leftover from that. The homemaking career is a question of *self-education*. Self-education is a sign of modern humanity.

Forming the Household Individually

Humanity is changing. A time has begun in which the movement towards the spirit originates with the individual. In this regard the homemaking career plays a new and modern role. For a career is indicated in which everything depends on self-education.

Self-education is characteristic of modern education. Whereas in the old paths of learning students were often dependent upon a teacher, the human being today relies on himself.

Rudolf Steiner speaks of this independence in his book *The Philosophy of Spiritual Activity*. The human being should determine the basis for his existence himself. Every path of development today rests on the self-formation of the human being. For centuries the human being was determined from without. Rudolf Steiner's book *Knowledge of the Higher Worlds and its Attainment* begins with a tremendous sentence: 'He will discover how he should try to do this or that exercise according to his particular individuality.' This is a new point of departure. The teacher becomes an advisor; he does show the pupil exercises, but he doesn't tell him how he should practise. The career of homemaking stands right in the middle of this new situation. The homemaker has to find out for herself how to form her own household.

The individual form is valid also for the aspect of time. Time holds a great source of strength in it, if we can only discover it. The human being lives in time-processes—days, weeks, years. We structure life by *forming* time.

Essentially human life is divided into three parts: work, sleep and free time. Things and necessities of all kinds make demands on the human being in work; while sleeping he is given over to nature's processes. Between work and sleep he is free; that is the so-called leisure time. That is where the human being can form his life individually. The home-maker works with this space. Her work makes free time possible for the members of the family.

The working day of a homemaker differs from that of other working people. If for example someone works 40 hours and sleeps 56 hours, that leaves him about 72 hours weekly for the home. The homemaker doesn't have this clear division.

Rhythm

Rhythm is strength. And strength arises where time and life are formed rhythmically. Nature determines the rhythmic forming of time sequences. Nature takes the human being through the seasons. The great rhythms of nature in which the human being is placed are there already. The human being can only win his own strength if within the greater rhythms he finds his own. For by rhythmically repeating an activity one creates a kind of platform in the etheric element; one secures something in the etheric element where otherwise one would have nothing on which to stand. And one day one will be able to throw one's glance into the spiritual world from this place—Rudolf Steiner describes it like this.

This is why even the smallest exercise—and even if it were only to look out of the window each evening—becomes a source of strength: rhythm is strength. Whoever recognizes this handles his day in a different way.

Family life brings a certain rhythm with it already. The question is: can the day's events which arise of their own accord be formed further? Can little pauses be placed that emphasize the rhythm?

The same question is valid for weekly rhythms. How for example can a rhythmic emphasis be given to the seventh day?

A further source of strength are the festivals. But what is a festival actually? A festival makes a caesura in the course of the year. It is a moment determined by something that does not have an everyday quality. We turn away from work in order to turn towards the spirit, the divine, the spiritual. Sunday was the first festival day, for 'Sunday should be a day of rest'.

Festivals differ. Traditional festivals such as Christmas, Easter or the festival of St John are formed with the help of traditions. Individual festivals such as birthdays are formed individually. Festivals include joy and cheerfulness, but also seriousness. They are organisms composed of a number of components. These organisms are actually sources of strength for returning to everyday life refreshed. Festivals are sources both of inspiration and of strength. The old saying 'Rhythm is strength' is underlined by the celebration of the festivals, in which the emphasizing of the rhythmic element becomes a source of creativity and strength.

The course of each day, too, should have repeated moments of joy. This can sometimes appear utterly prosaic: the homemaker who allows herself a moment of rest with a cup of coffee and a cigarette; the child who looks forward to a story every evening before bed.

The human being creates such moments of joy for himself instinctively. It is one of the greatest secrets of life: to form the course of events so that time neither presses nor depresses but becomes a source of strength and inspiration.

There are no boundaries to personal imagination here. Such moments can be different in every family. What is essential is that these become rhythmic accents in everyday life. For nothing is more crushing than monotony. A rhythmic accent to life brings colour and makes working easier.

Life is tension. Tension arises through contrasting elements. If we succeed in moving rhythmically within this tension, then strength will arise.

Cultural Life

Where do we find a basis for human relationships in our current culture? This clearly is in the household. It used to be the village, the city or the country that was the carrier of culture. People lived together in the same village sharing the same culture, the same belief, and celebrating the same festivals. Today's society is pluralistic. People with different cultures and the most varying views live next to one another. If we speak of culture we can no longer refer to a large community. That is why the home has become the bearer of culture.

This is new in human history. An exception was Judaism after the Diaspora. When the Jews were driven out of Israel, the Jewish household with its celebration of the Sabbath became the bearer of their culture. In the synagogue they met and still do meet for prayer, but the home is where their whole Jewish life occurred and still does occur. The Jews are exemplary in this respect. With the support of their household customs they were able to preserve their culture even in heterogeneous surroundings.

In the meantime this has become the lot of humanity generally: the household is the carrier of culture, because that is where culture is developed. Family and household have thus become the kernel of the new Mystery culture. Culture cannot be ordered from above. The state can at most create the conditions that allow culture to arise. But culture has to be borne out by people.

Cultural life includes what the human being does in the realm of knowledge, science, art and the religious-social life. So where do we find culture in the household? A bit of culture may be cultivated with literature, for example. The first step into science begins with the child's first picture book. Art begins with the first drawing. Music, modelling and painting are cultural elements within the household.

And where do we find the religious-social element? Towards the end of his life Rudolf Steiner used the expression 'social life' more and more instead of 'religion' in speaking of the trinity 'science, art and religion'. For social life is the main thing with regard to religion. Religion begins with the small child, which by nature is a religious being. Prayers belong in this category, but prayer should not be forced. It would also be pointless to pray with the children if the parents don't do it themselves. For children can tell whether something is imposed on them or whether it comes out of their parents' own self-understanding. The truth always has a better effect than a lie.

The same is true for the artistic element. One cannot demand artistic activities of the children if the parents don't do it themselves. This should make it clear: the entire culture of a family must rest on truth.

How much culture is justified in a family? The children teach their mother here; for children reveal their needs honestly. Here there is still an unbelievable amount to learn and discover. The important thing is that the homemaker look at the facts freely without prejudice and then herself decide what is right for her family. If someone comes and says how something should be done, then he is not speaking out of anthroposophy. For anthroposophy is only a matter of portraying a fact, with its conditions and laws; the other person should be left free to align himself with it or not—that is a maxim of Rudolf Steiner.

Only when an honest and true cultural life is realized within the family will civilization thrive. To say it differently: all of the aids achieved by our civilization should be used, but these aids are only justified if the human being freed thereby now unfolds a life of culture. That should finally constitute the freedom of the human being.

Culture always had (and still has) two sides. On the one hand certain cultural duties in the religious realm had to be fulfilled; they included church songs and sacred buildings, the striving for knowledge, and religious-social behaviour. A new polarity was added at the end of the Middle Ages and the beginning of the present: culture became more and more—out of a middle-class attitude—entertainment, pleasure. Once a duty ordered from above, culture now served the egoistic satisfaction of wishes. The transition to the middle-class way of living—in a negative sense—reduced our cultural life to fun and amusement. The homemaker must find a middle way between Scylla and Charybdis—or, in anthroposophical terms, between Ahriman and Lucifer. But what is it?

Friedrich Schiller characterized this middle in his work *On the Aesthetic Education of Man*. There he speaks of two polarities: the form impulse, which causes what people create to freeze into form, and the material impulse, which gives it substance. Neither element can be human, for only play is human: 'For, to say it for once, the human being only plays when he is a human being in the full sense of the word, and he is only then completely human when he plays.'

If one thinks here not of children's play, but of the 'play of free forces', then the element of play—now no longer under the force of form or matter—unfolds freely; play unfolds in such a way that the human being experiences freedom while engaged in it. This is what Schiller meant with his idea of the 'playing human being'.

Related to the household this means that the cultural life of the home should be imbued neither with force nor with egoistic pleasure; it should be determined by free play.

The Path of Development of the Homemaker

In what has been said until now ideals have been characterized again and again. In reality, however, these ideals indicate sources of strength. For what happens in the household is a piece of human culture. All this culminates eventually in the path of development of the homemaker. The homemaker appears to have only little time for her path of development. But there are quiet moments even in the household day. In these phases—however short they may be—the homemaker can begin the path of development that will gradually change her existence. Such a path has two aspects: *the meditative life and the exercises.*

'Wisdom is only in truth' is a basic meditative sentence by Rudolf Steiner. Of course one can meditate on a different sentence. Important is only that the meditative sentence has a content that one can think about. Meditation causes the world to become more transparent; the human being begins to see certain things between and behind the physical things.

What are the exercises, the other part of the path? The prime exercise is the concentration exercise. One endeavours for five minutes to arrest the continual fluctuation of the thoughts by thinking about an uninteresting object. As one tries to enter into a process with this, imaginations may arise.

Exercises and meditation belong together. The one does not work without the other: schooling of the will in the exercises, deepening of the heart forces in meditation. There are, however, countless meditations and exercises. One of them is the attitude: 'Learn to distinguish between the essential and the inessential.' This thought meets exactly the problem of the homemaker—all day long essential and inessential things are mixed into her day. If the homemaker reminds herself daily of what is essential, then a force will grow within her, a force organ. This force will enable her to take up the essential elements in the course of the day while leaving inessentials aside.

Why do people often lack strength? Because they give their efforts to inessentials just as much as to essentials. There are homemakers who can run a household in a completely relaxed way. They know exactly what is important: first take care of what is important. The question of what is essential can be asked in many ways. Important is that it be asked at all.

With the following six basic exercises (described by Rudolf Steiner as 'supplementary exercises') everyday attributes are practised. Along with the attitude exercise they form the basis for the homemaker's career.

The first exercise consists in doing the *concentration exercise* mentioned above, for about two weeks. If one combines it with the meditation 'Differentiate between essentials and inessentials' then one will develop a strong force.

A second exercise is the *initiative exercise*. For two weeks one does a certain act each morning and evening. The action should not be determined by outer necessities, for the point of the exercise is to choose something that arises out of one's own will, one's own intentions.

A third exercise has to do with *equanimity*. One should hold back all expressions of feeling for a short time (not the feeling themselves!). This exercise can of course only be practised at certain moments, when equanimity is appropriate.

The *positivity exercise* is purely and simply the homemaker's exercise. Rudolf Steiner illustrates it with the following story. Christ is walking with his disciples. They see a partially decayed dead dog. The disciples turn away from the horrible sight, but Christ says: what beautiful teeth the animal has! The exercise thus consists in finding something positive in everything.

A fifth exercise has to do with *freedom from bias*. One should try to 'develop in oneself the feeling of approaching every new experience totally without prejudice', at every moment one must 'be ready to accept a totally new experience'.

The sixth exercise is the matter of *persistence*. One should try to 'repeat all five exercises again and again systematically in regular turns. In this way a beautiful balance is gradually achieved in the soul...One gains a quiet understanding of things that previously were totally closed to the soul. Even the gait and the gestures of a person change under the influence of such exercises...' (see Rudolf Steiner, *Esoteric Development*).*

Sacramentalism

The five-thousand-year-long Dark Ages have come to an end; a new Age of Light is beginning. In it the homemaker, indeed the household itself, will gain a totally new meaning. Rudolf Steiner expressed this with the word 'sacramentalism'. In a lecture from the cycle *The Karma of Vocation* (27 November 1916) in which he speaks of the spiritual background of careers, he says that 'sacramentalism' should be brought into our practical lives: 'If in whatever the human being does he has the consciousness that Christ is behind him, and that he should do nothing else in the world except those things that he can do with Christ's help, this is progressing towards sacramentalism...What used to be fostered symbolically in the old Christian cults must now take hold of the whole world; what used to happen only on the altar must now take hold of the whole world. Humanity must learn to treat nature just as the gods themselves used to treat it ... to fulfil a holy service in everything, bring sacramentalism into everything.'

Let us take this word 'sacramentalism' seriously, turning

*New York: Anthroposophic Press 1982.

our attention again to the household. Activities of culture and civilization are concentrated there; everything is mirrored there. There the homemaker can work to make our society more spiritual.

'Social work will become a sacrificial service, it will be a continuation of the old cultic services.' (See Rudolf Steiner, *First Steps in Supersensible Perception*, 18 November 1922.)* Religion in its old form will continue for a long time still. But something new is beginning: a *general* priesthood. Every human being will become a priest, and everyone will treat the earth in a sacrificial way. As grave as this may sound, neither joy nor cheerfulness are exempted from it; religion can be permeated with joy.

What is the task of the homemaker in this new situation? She becomes a priestlike figure, she takes over a priestly function. The idea 'priesthood' can easily be misunderstood here, but it must be used to indicate the direction meant. One should not think of traditional priestesses, but of a type that existed in the ancient Mysteries—an Isis priestess, or the ancient priestesses of the Mystery cultures that still were part of matriarchal societies. Only when the homemaker sees herself as a new type of priestess can life in the household be understood as a sacrament and so become a seed for the new Mystery culture. Ultimately this means that the work of the homemaker will gradually become permeated with spirit, that she will understand it as something spiritual. Spirituality is everywhere.

This insight rises up as a great ideal of mankind, far beyond the ideal of the homemaker alone. But if the homemaker asks herself why she was incarnated into this life, she will receive a kind of certainty: she is living it because a new value will arise with this work; she is living this life because through her homemaker existence a priestly force arises that was active throughout the work of

*London: Anthroposophical Publishing Company 1949.

the priestesses of ancient times. The homemaker is standing at the point where something is changing, where something must change, if our whole civilization and culture are not to be lost.

4
Questions

How could one describe the work of the homemaker? Where do her responsibilities lie?

The household is manifold. Everything having to do with being human plays a role here and demands its appropriate place. Think of food and hygiene; of assistance to the young and the old; of everything that connects the human being with the spirit—continuing education, artistic elements or the religious life. In between there is the broad area of soul activity taken up by entertainment and play, etc. For all of these areas the homemaker carries responsibility.

But it must be repeated: the homemaker does not have an orderly work week like other working people. For a working person, a week of 168 hours divides into 40 hours of working time, 56 hours of sleeping time, with 72 hours remaining for the home. The homemaker, however, cannot withdraw to the home after a 40-hour week. On the contrary, she must be present during the 72 hours of free time belonging to her husband and children. If we therefore add these 72 hours to the 40 hours, her work time is 112 hours. This extended number of hours shows just how important this area is and how much human substance and strength the homemaker invests in it.

What is the significance of free time?

As a rule a person will form his free time according to his own impulses. Rudolf Steiner suggested that an artistic form could be given to the most varied areas of life—that we develop an art of living.

Thus the human being can form his own biography.

Here facts of the outer biography, training and experience, play a role as do inner qualities. The inner biography often unfolds unseen and completely independently of the outer factors. The best opportunities for bringing inner and outer biography together are in the home. There the human being lives free of outer demands. He can open himself for the spirit there. If Rudolf Steiner states in his book *Occult Science* that all higher knowledge has to do with being able to carry waking consciousness more and more over into sleep, so everything that the human being undertakes in this direction, everything that brings to life the elements of a path of knowledge in him, everything that consciously brings the spirit into his biography comes about because his free time has been formed to make space for a meditative life. If his inner life is deepened here in this middle realm, then his impulses for action will arise here also. How he places himself into the objective world of work, what he can offer there—all of this comes from the area that is described in *Faust* by the words: 'Here I am a human being, here I may be human.'

The household has changed. Who can still imagine a household without the media and without technical aids? What are the consequences? How should the homemaker deal with them?

Only if it is studied individually in each case can the effect on the human being be found. But this should not be done with an attitude of rejection. These things cannot be banned from the world. That would only be putting oneself on an island and making oneself blind to what is going on. One needs to know what is happening in the world. It cannot be a matter of rejecting an instrument such as the computer. The thing to do is to perceive it, understand how it works, and then apply it accordingly. In this way specific forces can be developed and set against the harmful influences.

'Creating a balance': how can something of the spiritual realm be set against subnature?

Rudolf Steiner did not say we should reject things, avoid them or shut them out. It is much rather a case of carefully looking at them until they reveal their nature and their effect. Only thus can a state of balance be won anew. An example Rudolf Steiner mentioned was reading the newspaper. If one observes oneself exactly one notices that something of the nature of the deadly nightshade is connected with it—then one can start looking for something to compensate for it.

Such compensating forces can only be found with real spiritual science—a spiritual science which does not stop at opinions and thoughts, but which does research, making concrete descriptions, right down to the finest differentiations. Anthroposophical spiritual science is exceedingly difficult. But if one makes it one's own, then just in overcoming the difficulties forces are developed which may not be noticed until difficult problems need to be solved. Then one may notice that one does find a way of dealing with them. Whoever really studies anthroposophy becomes practical in life.

Anthroposophy wants to penetrate the world and man with thoughts, to understand how the spirit works. In some points anthroposophy has achieved a kind of 'intermediate level of research' that is most inadequate in meeting the demands of the rapidly developing media. For we do not fully understand the harmful influence of the most complicated electrical machines; thus also we have drawn no comprehensive picture of how to compensate for them. This is an important task for anthroposophy: to create a force that will compensate for the inroad of subnature.

Is the same true for the use of technical aids?

A homemaker who wants to do justice to her task will not

have the tendency to dismiss things; she will be inclined to bring them into balance. She used to do things by hand. This meant that her work was permeated with spirit, with soul, with life. Today these activities are more and more replaced by forces that come from subnature.

The household organism, which used to be permeated by human activity, is being pressed back more and more, replaced with the technical effects of the sub-sense world—with electricity and magnetism.

The instinctive consciousness that had been carrying the housework was not equal to this invasion by the technical world. The totally ruined circumstances of family life reveal this. Inhuman things carrying out our household tasks caused a peculiar desolation; the ego can no longer support the elements of desolation within the soul, and they have thus created a crass counter-picture to the characteristic family of the previous century.

What are the consequences?

The career profile of a person responsible for the home must be sketched anew. The actual reason for the collapse lies in the fact that the homemaker's career involves a sphere that includes the whole breadth of human existence. This sphere of work can no longer be developed by instinct; it must occur through understanding.

What steps can we take towards understanding?

First of all the elements need to be brought to mind that are of importance in a household—from cleaning to praying. In a second step the relationship of the elements to one another needs to be observed. How do they relate to one another? Where is the emphasis? What processes are going on? In the foreground stands the fact that every element is surrounded by a soul component. Will we play Chinese checkers or cards, will the children be put to bed or is it time to clean—

every activity submits to a different mood. The problem is that we live abstractly and think we can do different things in the same mood. That does not do justice to the individual elements.

One also does not do justice to the elemental beings. What do they expect from us?

Consciousness! Every thought is a reality—a good one or a bad one. Hateful thoughts directed towards a person harm him; loving thoughts do him some good. If one has thoughts that relate to the world of elemental beings in a valid way, then they receive something. They receive human substance, so to speak, for only the human being can form thoughts. They receive nourishment from the centre of their evolutionary situation. It is nourishment for them when human beings think of them and relate to them lovingly. Elemental beings are like children who dance and are happy if their mothers stroke their hair.

But for centuries elemental beings have been receiving less and less. The results of this are noticeable in the processes of death that have overcome nature in many places—in the dying forests for example. This trend is caused less by pollution than by the lack of attention paid to elemental beings. Human beings neglect them with the consequence that they turn to another world, the realm of death ruled by Ahriman. Because the human being doesn't give them anything any more the elemental beings are beginning to become ahrimanic.

So human beings have to pay more attention to elemental beings?

Human beings have to try to develop a knowing feeling and willing in the sense of the Age of the Consciousness Soul in order to once again give them what they need. Then they will be able to help human beings again. This fact is of such importance that Rudolf Steiner spoke of it, as if in a great sign of the times, in his last lecture at the Goetheanum (the fire which was to destroy it had already been lit): 'If this dying earth-existence is to be re-enlivened, carry impulses for the future, it can come about in no other way than it does in human beings, by the insertion of soul and spirit into mineral and vegetable elements' (see Rudolf Steiner, *Man and the World of the Stars*, 31 December 1922).* This process can begin in many places. But the elements that make up the community in a home are especially well suited to what the elemental beings seek.

How can the community within the home approach this elemental world?

A beginning is made when someone makes it his task to take every object into his hand in as attentive a way as possible and use it as if it were a living being. This is a long process. Mankind has become accustomed to viewing objects in a rational and functional way, which also influences how things are treated. This doesn't mean that one should become sentimental or sacrifice clarity. One can hit a nail with a hammer exactly and carefully and still express loving interest.

Everywhere we look is nature—thoughts of the gods. These thoughts—living elemental beings—had a relationship with human beings in the past. Now they want to enter into a relationship with human beings once again. If one takes some object seriously, one discovers that it arose through a process—it reveals a history. There are wonderful exercises for this. At lunch one can say for example: 'The salt is now Mr Salt. How does he look, this Mr Salt?' One can approach the creative elements of imagination in this way.

---

*New York: Anthroposophic Press 1963.

Speaking of 'salt': how can a relationship be found to foodstuffs?

Cleaning vegetables is not exactly a popular activity. Yet just this leads one directly into the elemental world. If a carrot is scraped or scrubbed, a potato peeled or washed, elemental beings are freed. Elemental beings live in transitions. If light falls on a crystal, if water from a spring drips onto a stone, undines come into being there. They do not live an individual life but find their sense of life, their sense of satisfaction, in coming into being. Thus washing vegetables calls forth an unpleasant feeling in the human being, and a pleasant one in the elemental beings. Then the vegetables are cut, a sympathetic activity for human beings; the elemental beings, however, feel that they are being divided, which is an unsympathetic experience for them. For them this is pain connected with becoming free. If one eats an apple, the difference between a slice of apple and a whole apple is noticeable. Just so one has a natural sense for not simply cutting into a living body; one knows what pain this can cause. These feelings for the material world must be rediscovered and developed.

From materials to people: to truly understand the human being, one has to remember that he has gone through various earth lives. How does reincarnation affect the household?

The human being is divided into a head and a limb being, both imbued with the rhythmic system. The rhythmic system provides a basis for our life of feeling. The will is at home in our metabolic-limb system, and thinking depends on our nerve-sense-system. Now, the human being underwent a previous incarnation some time ago. At that time he had the same makeup as he will have again after he has died—after he has gone into the spiritual world—and reincarnated. Three such incarnations are connected in terms of the constitution. What our limbs radiate today, what goes out into the world from them, what our will-ego is, that is the ego which was formed by our thinking in our previous incarnation. There we thought about the world, we developed impulses for freedom. Our current knowledge is not yet truly the ego of the present; it is once again an ego in becoming. From it will emerge what will live in our will in a future incarnation. Between them lives our actual ego of the present, our rhythmic (feeling) system.

Thus we are surrounded by our ego in a threefold way. This makes it clear that the ego is not a point but an extremely differentiated time being. If we look at someone, we always see his past incarnation in the revelation of his will. But his future incarnation is being prepared already in his thinking and knowing. These two elements, the will-ego of the past incarnation and the becoming ego of the future one, combine in all that is the feeling human being in the widest sense, the character of the present ego.

All of these connections play into the home community.

What does this mean for a mother who feels responsible in a karmic sense? How can she solve the question of 'why'?

Different exercises allow one to approach these questions. Important first of all is that one be extremely cautious personally, that one practise intense self-control. One must never speculate with regard to questions of karma. As a general rule, when carrying out Rudolf Steiner's karma exercises, pictures rise up that one would never have expected.

A first exercise. No household runs without a hitch. Apparent chance mishaps, incidents and unplanned events will occur constantly. The exercise consists in imagining a little human being behind everything that happens. Rudolf Steiner expressly says that this is a kind of thought experiment. Nevertheless the imagined human form will suddenly become reality. The more intensively one does the exercise, the stronger becomes the relationship to this being:

it becomes a part of oneself. This means that when all is said and done, one has created the difficulties oneself.

In doing a karma exercise we should be aware of the basic idea of karma. We are here to do a self-chosen task, to learn from doing it. We incarnate in order to make progress. That is why we create difficulties for ourselves in life. Part of our astral being is continually working to enable exactly those things to occur which will enable our forces to develop. This part of our astral being begins to become perceptible through this first karma exercise.

A second exercise can follow after a fairly long time. In life we always stand in unwanted situations. For a home-maker these are concentrated. The exercise is to imagine that we actually wanted all these unwanted moments. In recognizing that such a situation has been created we ask ourselves who created it, and we come to the thought that we ourselves wanted it. If we think in this way then a reality reveals itself. We begin to take steps in the world which we did not even know existed.

A third exercise consists in remembering an event of the day each evening, perhaps a conversation. We try to picture it exactly. Where did I stand, where was the other person? What was each of us wearing? How did the light fall on our faces? What was said? Rudolf Steiner recommended that we really dig ourselves in, exerting ourselves as if we would actually chew the pencil, to get it all pictured vividly.

A last question. Why are home communities so significant?

No one can be alone. The most important motif is the sentence: 'Where two or more are gathered in Christ's name, He can be among them.' The solitary person alone cannot find Christ.

The entire mysteries of the consciousness soul begin to light up with such a thought. A community is there because its members give something to each other. It is there because it is the path of the new age—towards a true life in spirit. At the same time it is a true experience of the Christ Being. In anthroposophy we speak of how the Christ Being is entering into a totally new relationship with the human being at the end of the century. He is becoming the Lord of Karma. He did not used to be. Until recently a different being stood in His place, a being working totally from out of the past, one who represented the Father God—Moses. Moses determined the law: what you have done in one life you must compensate for in the next. What you gave comes back to you; it is a law.

The Moses being stepped back. Christ took his place. He is beginning to form the karma of humanity in freedom and love—in view of what will be beneficial to all of humanity—by means of the destinies of individual human beings. Moses would have said: you must suffer your destiny, even if it is harmful for everyone around you. Christ's language transforms this into: you should experience in your destiny what is beneficial for your surroundings.

An anthroposophical home community is a place in which the influence of Christ can best take hold: here space can be created through inner mobility and openness.